CULTURES OF THE WORLD! UNITED KINGDOM, SPAIN & FRANCE

CULTURE FOR KIDS
CHILDREN'S CULTURAL STUDIES BOOKS

PROFESSOR GUSTO
EDUCATIONAL & INFORMATIVE BOOKS FOR CHILDREN
(PRE-K / K-12)

What do you know about the British, Spanish and French Cultures?

If you want to understand people better, studying their cultures can help. Learning a person's culture is a basic introduction to the person's identity.

BRITISH CULTURE

The United Kingdom's capital is London. Its government is a constitutional monarchy. Although there is no constitutionally-identified official language, English is the main language spoken by more than 70% of the UK population.

Scotland

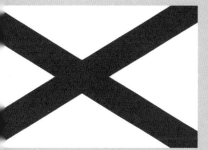

rthern Ireland

Wales

England

The United Kingdom is composed of four countries. They are England, Scotland, Wales, and Northern Ireland. Each area has a strong sense of national identity and culture.

In the past, people have had greater access to higher education. Wealth inequality is increasing. We can say that the British class system is still intact. British class is simply not about wealth or where one lives. It is based more on complex factors like demeanor, accent, manners, and assumptions.

The British are known for their stiff upper lip and their blitz spirit. In the face of adversity or embarrassment, the "keep calm and carry on" attitude still lives on today. British are contained in their body language and gestures when they speak. Even if they want to be friendly, they may seem a bit closed.

The common greeting of British people is the handshake. They seem to be formal and stiff in conversation. They feel uncomfortable if eye contact is prolonged. The British enjoy entertaining people in their homes. Their table manners are continental, so the fork is held in the left hand and the knife in the right while eating.

SPANISH CULTURE

Spain is known for its flamenco music and dance. Bullfights also add color to its rich culture.

Spain is gifted with majestic beaches and beautiful sunshine. But Spain has more to offer than that. For hundreds of years, Spain was one of the cultural centers in Europe.

Spain is widely known for its extraordinary artistic heritage. Well-known figures of the Golden Age are El Greco and Diego Velasquez. Francisco de Goya was Spain's most renowned artist. He worked in the 18th century.

In the early 20th century, the art world was greatly influenced by a remarkable group of Spanish artists. These include Pablo Picasso and Juan Gris. Prehistoric monuments in Minorca, the Roman ruins of Merida and Tarragona, Gothic cathedrals, and castles are just some of Spain's impressive architecture.

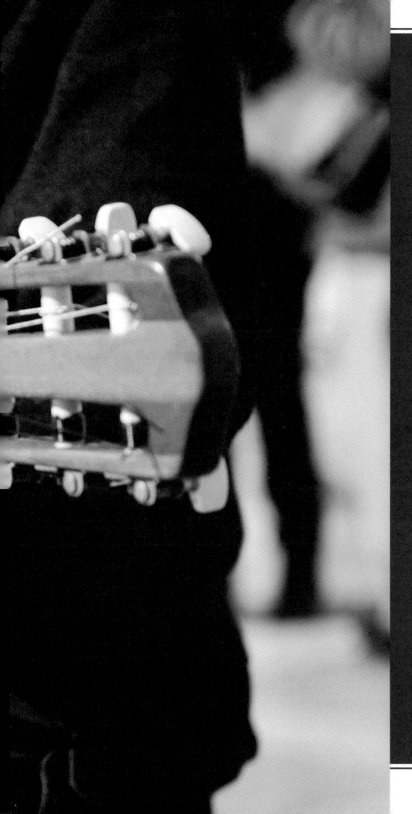

The invention of the Spanish guitar is one of the most important parts of the culture in Spain. This was invented in Andalusia in the 1790's. Its modern shape was gained in the 1870's. Musicians around the world have used this guitar to give the world pleasure.

FRENCH CULTURE

French culture is associated with Paris, the nation's capital. It is the center of fashion, cuisine, art and architecture. Actually, the word culture comes from France. It is derived from the Latin word "colere". The term means to tend and nurture the earth.

French is the official language of the country's 66 million residents. It is also the first language of 88% of the population. In fact, the second most widely learned foreign language in the whole world is French.

The predominant religion of France is Catholicism. About 64% of the population are Roman Catholics. They are usually offended by any negative comments about their country. Foreign visitors can often interpret their attitude as rude.

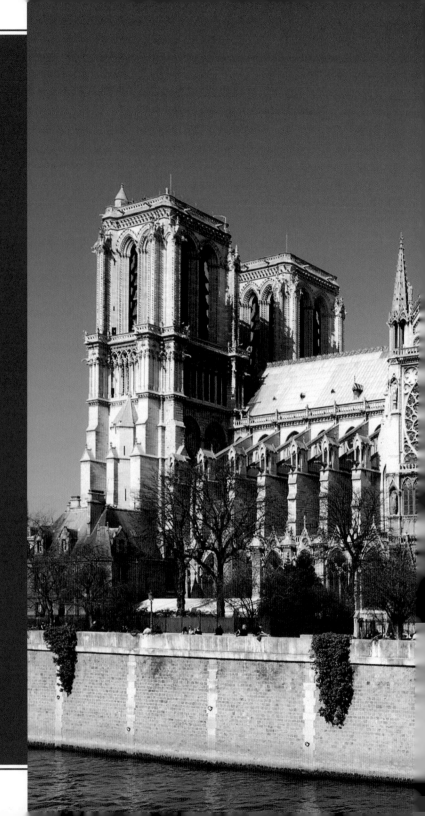

The expression "chauvinism" originated in France. The term means an attitude that members of your own gender are always better than those of the opposite sex. It also refers to the belief that your country or race is better than any others.

The home to many high-end fashion houses is Paris. French people are known for their sophisticated, professional and fashionable style of dress. Nice dresses, suits, long coats, scarves and berets characterize their typical outfits.

Among the world's largest museums in Paris is the Louvre Museum. It is a home to many famous words of art. The famous Mona Lisa and Venus de Milo are in it.

The traditional Christian holidays of Christmas and Easter are also celebrated in France. May 1 in France is Labor Day. July 14 is Bastille Day, remembering the day the Bastille prison in Paris was stormed by revolutionaries in 1789.

Printed in Great Britain
by Amazon